CRACKED SKULL CINEMA

DAVID BRIGGS

Cracked Skull Cinema

SALT

CROMER

PUBLISHED BY SALT PUBLISHING 2019

2 4 6 8 10 9 7 5 3 1

First published in Great Britain in 2019 by
Salt Publishing Ltd
12 Norwich Road, Cromer, Norfolk NR27 0AX United Kingdom

www.saltpublishing.com

Salt Publishing Limited Reg. No. 5293401

A CIP catalogue record for this book is available from the British Library

ISBN 978 1 78463 207 6 (Paperback edition)

Typeset in Sabon by Salt Publishing

Printed and bound in Great Britain by Clays Ltd, Elcograf S.p.A

for Forrest, Wolf, Ernst, and Auden

Contents

'There is a crack in everything;
that's how the light gets in.'

LEONARD COHEN

CRACKED SKULL CINEMA

Late Electric Age

Simply to be breaking even in those days
was to feel like that man you spoke of once who,

when The Great Crash came on cue, found himself
among the swells, quaffing rum and crème de cacao
    cocktails,

smoking Havanas, admiring his host's apartment –
its towering bookcase, ebony cabinet, wall-mounted antlers –

not entirely sure how he'd landed on this last island
of decadence, among the cockroaches, while civilisation

crackled to a stub outside: the bombs loud, but distant,
still, on the gone side of town. The corona

of his host's cigar seemed infernal, in the way luxury
cheek-by-jowl with genocide can seem to emit a whiff

of the Mephitic, and especially to good little Puritan boys
from the suburbs who've snagged their trews

on the thorns of privilege and haven't a clue
how to unhook themselves. So, when the electric went finally

all he could say was, 'I guess I'd better light a candle
in the darkness,' while lighting a candle in the darkness,

and everyone laughed because the mimesis of word
and action seemed somehow faintly charming.

Five Lessons

after W S Graham

I

So, Karl, you know my reputation
and you come seeking to master the guitar.
I haven't invited you to sit. Stand
at the window, there, and sing what you see.
If we're to spend the time fruitfully
I must ascertain not so much the dexterity
of your fingers as the clarity of your vision.
Sing, I said. And make it the tune
of what's out there in the street,
not the tired strains of your callow mind's
incessant and predictable soundscape.
Sing me the fleas on the homeless soldier's dog,
the flagging ennui of shopworkers,
acidic graffiti, moss in the window rubber
of abandoned cars. Sing
just one thing true,
and we'll begin.

II

I know you're keen to demonstrate your skill,
Karl, but let's return briefly to first principles.
Consider the way a note vibrates in air.
To pluck this string, here,
is to discompose the air around it,
and why should we wish to do that
unless we are certain the disruption we intend

will move all those within its range
to weep like a hit-and-run driver
in the immediate, whisky-wet aftermath.
Your first note is the first word
of your manifesto, the first brick
through the window of Parliament.
It requires not only a sure grip,
but absolute dedication
to the conscious disturbance of air.

III

In this, your third lesson,
I should like you to compare the bars
of this lacquered fretboard
to Jacob's ladder as seen by Milton's Satan
from the purlieus of Chaos, at the edge
of created space. See how my fingers
scale the rungs like angelic messengers
between worlds. It's not enough, Karl,
simply to position your fingertips;
they must be always moving with the graceful
    precision
of Raphael on God's stairwell, earthbound
to warn Adam of the precarious nature
of his as yet unfathomed condition.
You may practise without picking
while I finish this letter to my patron.

IV

As I have explained, Karl, a chord
is a pattern of waves lapping
against the ear, and to conjure it
we must become both wind and seabed,
and the fetch between continents.
Do not return till you have learned
to sound each chord so true
your audience swears it hears seabirds
between each root and minor third,
till they speak of feeling salt-spray
spit through each perfect fifth.

V

Karl, it is good to see progress,
but I believe we've reached an impasse.
I have known for some time I must say this.
Your position in society
is a near insurmountable impediment
to absolute mastery of the guitar.
You fit too comfortably in a world
designed by and for people largely like you.
This is to say, for all your burgeoning skill
you lack grit. You play competently,
without soul, and I fear
our time together has run its course.
Should you commit to a precarious life
of uncertain means, in pursuit of your art,

you may, in time, accrue enough of suffering
to supply the present deficiency.
This is your choice. I cannot say.
Please leave today's fee on the bureau, there.
I trust you understand me when I wish you
nothing but heartbreak, injustice,
ignominy and pain.

Ljubljana

Walking home through the park there's a man
in a green t-shirt that says 'Ljubljana',
and for some inexplicable reason it strikes me
that I must pay attention to this sign –
in much the same way that the hapless protagonist
of a Russell Hoban novel might pay attention
to the shifting signs of his daily routine
as they begin to unveil a tantalising glimpse
of alternative realities behind the quotidian,
realities of which he'd hitherto been ignorant.

Later, reading Žižek on my balcony, I flip
to the blurb, where I read that Žižek
is, among many things, Senior Researcher
at the University of Ljubljana,
and a quiver like a slammed door shaking the walls
of an entry-level Barratt home upsets my spine.

So I make tea. But before it brews I zip
around the corner to the Co-op to buy milk,
wherein the mother of a former student
tells me Jim's doing well, is travelling,
had been slacklining in sundry European capitals
till he fell and broke his leg in Ljubljana.

And now I'm uneasy, like Cary Grant in *North by
    Northwest*
making a scene in that bright hotel lobby

to get himself arrested and thereby sidestep
the Russian spies he's convinced are in pursuit,
whom he cannot expose as no-one'll believe him.

The camera shows us what Cary sees –
a gun-shaped protrusion from the lift-boy's pocket.
The spies see their prey using the cops to evade them.
The hotel guests, in their blinkered Eden,
enjoy the fallacy that nothing sinister is happening,
could ever happen, least of all here.
And Žižek suggests a fourth point-of-view,
that of the audience as indifferent Big Other
sadistically attuned to Grant's Noirish moment,
his existential solitude in the crowd.

Run away with me, reader. I've got two
one-way tickets for the next flight to Ljubljana.

Other People

I learned reluctantly to accept
those who'll never well up on a park bench

one leafwet November morning
at the maple-seed tailspin of existence;

those who'll never reckon the tally
of their contribution to human joy,

let alone consider themselves wanting;
those who've never found regret

at decades-gone acts of selfish stupidity
catching in their minds

like plastic bags in winter trees.
Imagine being them. Imagine the clarity

of minds like the unoccupied floors
in a harbourside office block,

with all its windows open,
and well-groomed men in singlets

on the anthracite carpet-tiles
doing squat-thrusts.

Vision Helmet

Simply by closing your eyes
you can don the Vision Helmet,
begin to see what's been peripheral
your whole life – a house with a porch
in a lakeside town, the smiling face
of your estranged child, the outline
of that poem you know you were born,
one day, to write – as it all heaves into view
like old friends at a reunion party.

Keep them closed. The visions keep coming:
firm-held hopes, long-cherished fears,
everything you never really knew you wanted
until, last of all, embroidered in yellow,
blue and red – Sitting Bull's moccasins.
The Sioux believed you should save
your best shoes for when you're dead.

In The Old Neighbourhood

I

SATURDAY AFTERNOON

Turning the corner you hope it's unchanged,
that baskets of convolvulus still hang

from next door's balcony facia;
that Don's stepping out perpetually

from his cheesecake-coloured front door
in a new shirt, looking for love;

that Ralph's playing the same five bars
on his baby grand in the hall-floor flat.

And there's that bench where you decided,
remember: ditching the present,

Dutching the future,
letting it all through your fingers

just as you might unclutch palmfuls of sand,
or how (years later) seeing loneliness

in the mirror nuzzle your shoulder,
you'll let fall a vase of narcissi, wait –

indefinitely – to hear it smash
on the hard, indifferent fact

that the past cannot be re-lived.

II

SATURDAY NIGHT

The barman fixes you an Old Fashioned.
The guy rapping at the open mic

cedes to a white-haired dude in muscle-tight t-shirt
on vox and blues harmonica;

the drummer of an old friend's band
wheels a floor tom through, parting a scrum

of Converse All-Stars and Ramones t-shirts.
Sixteen years since you were here

and nothing much seems to have changed,
except that your back aches from standing

and you're baffled by the washroom graffiti.
Back in the bar, Father Time's asleep,

slumped over a half-empty rocks glass
at his corner table. But that's okay.

It's a reunion after all and no-one,
you notice, seems inclined to wake him.

III

SUNDAY AFTERNOON

A few hours at the hospice.
Why you came.
Why you stay away.

IV

SUNDAY EVENING

And then you're snapping back to the road
from a thought of her that afternoon
in her birthday frock, barely able to speak,
being fed through a tube,
going to Carolina in her mind.

Steering wheel in hand, white lines ahead
like an inescapable prognosis –
amazed you've not crashed;
pinching your handbacks;

not entirely sure that this, now,
isn't some road of the mind
spooling to fade
behind bloodied eyeballs
in a cracked skull cinema
while the wheels of your upended car
spin slowly to a halt.
That crepuscular light maybe not, after all,
merely weather into which you are driving.

Creed

Times he's walked to the cornershop
telling himself he's 'visiting his tobacconist',

half-believing it's alchemy to name things,
transforming them in the alembic of his brain,

distilling sanguinity from the routine.
Pocketing his change, he'll promenade

thinking that some prefer to believe
it's the lark who wakes the sun,

trees that shepherd the winds,
our minds that dream our bodies.

Some thoughts are like Cretan boys
shaking out their arms on a bluff,

preparing to dive into the Aegean
with barely a ripple, again and again,

simply because they can.
"The mind is its own place, after all."

Milton said that, in his blindness,
through his teeth,

and through the victory songs
of less imaginative enemies.

Muse

And then I'd ask you to believe

that fixing the ideal martini
requires a measure of precision in
the gestalt analysis of your condition;

that I desire little more than to stir
over Kold Draft the perfect ratio of gin,
vermouth, and angostura, then

deftly squeeze a lemon twist
till three beads of oil
are floating on that lucid meniscus.

I'll pass it gently across the bar, knowing
the first taste will dissolve doubt,
the second revive faith in your powers,

the third unclose that door in your brain
behind which words, genius, and craft
effortlessly commingle.

the desk

he'd spend hours just   sitting at it
whole mornings   not thinking   not really
of anything   wet afternoons watching wind
through the window shutters   in its waltz
with the trees   in next door's garden

he'd positioned his writerly talismen   ink bottles
tarot pack   paperweight Hanuman
each had its place   and the booklined walls
of the room   in which the desk sat   were
book room red   his milk-white Eames chair

perfectly square   to the typewriter on the desk
sometimes he'd rise for a moment   to make
delicate adjustments to the rug   or the books
on the shelves   but then he'd return to the desk
and when the house   of which the room

around the desk was a part   required attention
of one kind or another   he begrudged it
everyday   the street containing
the   house   with   a   bookroom-red   room
around the desk   would hum away

at its enticing routines   in vain
the siren-voiced city itself   might threaten
to lure him back   into the undesky life
but he knew his station   they'd have to
get along without him   what he had to do was

[16]

keep turning up   keep watch at the desk
any   day   now   he'd   say   any   day   now
and having kept watch so faithfully   so long
he wasn't about to miss a shift   for how
he reasoned   would he ever forgive himself

if one truant lapse   happened to coincide
with the moment that   She   appeared
his long-desired burlesque girl   Truth
in her platform heels   and black silk corset
for a few dancing seconds   on the desk

Reader Response

After the reading, and the bit on the panel,
a red-haired librarian tells me about
a form of asceticism
among a lesser-known sect of sadhus
that involved lengthening the male member
by suspending from it
a protracted series
of incrementally heavier stones.
It must've taken some time, and not
an inconsiderable degree of commitment.

Legend has it, she says, that one such holy man
stepped out from a pulsing crowd
amassed for Victoria Regina
and into the path of the elephant parade,
the imperial howdah, to expose his
cultivated phallus to the Royal Gaze.

For him it must have been an article of faith
that the restricted point-of-view
of those blinkered by rank –
those who see darkly through veils of privilege,
who cannot see the world as it is,
cannot cope with too much reality –
can only be broken wide open
by means of a profound shock to the psyche.
Thus, the devout flasher performs
an act of consciousness expansion

more potent than your typical Anglican sermon.
And thus your royal majesty gets woke.

But what I'd like to be able to remember
is whether she's telling me this apocryphal story

i. apropos of nothing in particular,

   or

ii. by way of response to my poetry.

Somewhere in the Multiverse

While Yeats was famous for a raffish jiggle of the tortoiseshell handle of his rimless pince-nez, Gertrude Stein began by swinging an imaginary golf club, as though 'teeing off' into the audience. It's well known Beckett always swept downstage into warm applause to pose, ironically, in a couched side-profile posture not unlike Rodin's *The Thinker*; that Joyce couldn't stop firing his trademark gunfingers at the dress-circle balcony. Wyndham Lewis became predictable for sneering irritably at every pause or denouement, while Vita Sackville-West would hold her arm out horizontally to display a calligraphic tattoo of her favourite mantra. Basil Bunting would tap his chest then join his fingertips in a Valentine's heart, while Louis Zukofsky preferred to enter the stage from audience-centre-aisle at an energetic canter, then spin on one heel before delivering his set. And everyone remembers e e cummings for the way he'd cast the mic out above the heads in the front-row stalls then flick it back in like a fly-fishing line. It's legend now that Virginia Woolf advised Eliot and Pound against leaving the stage that final time in a skip-dance rendition of 'Bring Me Sunshine'.

Quiddity

words were stones
    they skimmed through the surf

        talking it out

        diminishing circles

figures on a beach
    watching a sunset

           [*correction*]

        not so much a sun*set*

optics

an illusion sustained

by the world's
    ceaseless
           spinning

Haecceity

not these rising in a cold glass of Champagne

nor those in the yellowy foam by the sewerage outlet

but these   now

blown from a plastic dipstick
            in a child's hand
                    on a spring breeze
                            into blue sky –

their fragile occupation of time

their fixed but futile desire

to hold their form

to maintain themselves awhile against

the unbearable pressure of space

Mythology

The doctor in *The Madness of King George* cures the king's porphyria-induced senility with a strong dose of irreverence – he looks at the king; the king is told he's 'merely the patient'; the king is restrained for misdemeanours and obscenities. And it's made clear that this Quakerish insolence is essential to the king's recovery.

In this way it is essentially the same film as *The King's Speech*, in which another oikish quack with a strong regional accent cures the king's inability to sound kingly by means of wilful disrespect.

And the appeal of these films must surely lie in the attractive idea that the renegade outsider with little respect for social distinctions is, in himself, the essential cure for the sickness at the heart of the establishment. *The Fisher King*. The little boy in *The Emperor's New Clothes*.

That, I guess, or their one other, lesser-spotted commonality – the under-sung prowess in the editing suite of BAFTA-award winning Tariq Anwar.

The Games We Play

after Francis Alÿs

His camera follows a ten-year-old boy
playing stick-and-wheel with a 35mm film reel
through the bomb-blown streets of Kabul.
The reel spins downhill, wheeling on its rim,
kept upright by the boy with his stick,
takes brief chickenesque flights
from the rocks and sewer-kerbs in its path
yet, somehow, always lands right;
keeps ticking its way past corrugated house fronts,
apartment blocks, bullet-holes in stonework,
smiling dudes in kefiyehs on antique Triumphs.
More street kids give chase, under a sun
like an automatic rifle's infra-red,
and the reel just keeps on rolling.

The whole thing's shot on handheld 35mm,
so there's an agreeable correspondence
between camera and subject, a correspondence
intended to provoke questions
about the function and purpose of film
in, and about, post-Bush/Blair Afghanistan.

I'm watching this in a big, white AC'ed room
in a gallery in Downtown Toronto.
The boy with the stick keeps running
after the unspooling reel
under a June-blue, drone-free sky,
through the mise-en-scène of a town
that's holding its breath
for the next big twist in the plot.

Teacups

Somewhere in Europe, in the eighteenth century,
someone added a handle to the small china tea bowl.
And someone put the first handle
on the small china teabowl
because tea was no longer being served tepid,
as in China, but hot.
And tea was now being served hot
to dissolve the refined cane sugar
everyone had started to spoon into it.
The latest thing.
And, in time, everyone
became addicted to the sudden
rush of refined cane sugar,
because it goes straight to the blood,
needles through organs we formerly used
to slowly break down the natural sugars
fermenting away in vegetables and fruits
and which, for aeons, before refined cane,
had been everyone's regular source.
And this rising demand for refined cane sugar
fuelled an increasing supply from the West Indies,
where someone had colonised the fertile land
in which sugar cane thrived,
and enslaved the people
by whom it was harvested.
And that someone dealt in slavery
because there was no law against it.
And there was no law against slavery
because centuries of assumed
racial and cultural superiority

had made almost everyone
supremely indifferent
to the humanity of anyone
not sitting politely
in a well-furnished drawing-room
deftly raising a bone-china teacup –
its handle poised
between soft, white fingers.

The Today Programme

Dyspeptic white men on the radio
interrogating dyspeptic white men
about the latest corruption scandal
involving dyspeptic white men.
Dyspeptic white men on the internet.
Dyspeptic white men calling their prejudice
common sense, as though it's Scripture,
in dyspeptic attacks on the politics
of those who aren't and won't ever be
dyspeptic white men.
Dyspeptic white men parroting headlines,
uncritically parroting headlines,
editorials and bylines commissioned,
written, printed, and distributed
by vain cartels of dyspeptic white men.
Dyspeptic white men voxpops.
Dyspeptic white men screaming incredulity
at any contentious enough to question
the Divine Right to Rule of dyspeptic white men.
The morally-bankrupt financial portfolios
of wealthy dyspeptic white men.
Dyspeptic white men with road rage,
rail rage, flight rage, screen rage.
Dyspeptic white men with screen rage
leering at laptops in online auctions
for trophy wives fetishistically thinner
than the first wives impoverished by divorce
from dyspeptic white men.
The dyspeptic scheming of dyspeptic white men.
Dyspeptic white men keeping things as they are –

a world perfectly calibrated for efficient production
of nothing but dyspeptic white men.

Newsworthy
for Jude

. . . and, finally, reports just in
suggest Angola may have fallen
through an Angola-shaped hole
in the news, and with it all hope
of making its mineral wealth pay;
of raising the portion of the millions
who live on less than $2 a day;
all hope of holding to account
the incumbent MPLA.
While Angola's cotton, coffee and cocoa
may well continue, for all we know,
to be hand-picked involuntarily
it is, we believe, now invisibly so
in that landmine-pocked limbo
on the dark side of the news.
It's possible still that Angola transforms
carbon into coal,
into diamonds harder
than the bloodshot stare
of its child-soldier veterans;
and that (by a similar alchemy)
the archetypal Angolan woman
is now less warrior-queen Nzinga
and more child-bride widow of UNITA.
Is it still news? our correspondent asks,
if Angola disappears and nobody hears?

Arboretum

Halfway through unquiet dreams
I found myself under the kale-green shade
of a hundred-year-old yew –

sheltering from the small rain
soaking the shagbark hickory and maples
out there in the wood. Elsewhere.

The scaffold branches horizontal,
then curving earthwards, furling
like tongues at their tips; each one thick

with laterals – bristling, pin-thin leaves.
You could prick your thumb.
Sleep a hundred years.

Sun through clouds grey as corridors
in the insomniac hospital;
grey clouds speeding far above now

like elsewhere-bound traffic.
And the cypresses shimmy with each gust,
their sequins flaming. Las Vegas showgirls.

But the common yew squats,
silent in the midst of less serious trees.
And I'll pass my time as she suggests –

say my one small thing clearly
to anyone who'll listen.
Keep saying it till her roots extend

to cork me among the unsleeping dead.

Untitled

Unrecorded, unacknowledged, unremembered,
the ghosts of the people swept to their graves
by the Mont Blanc fountain pens
of narcissist dictators
are staring through Eternity's windows,
able to do precisely nothing.

Forever condemned to watch the world's injustice:
those who orchestrate financial meltdown;
those who sign orders for shovels of quicklime
into unmarked mass graves,
as they peacock about on flashbulb-bright podiums
in full dress-uniform,
receiving another spurious medal.

But the dead are ghost-fingered.
Their ghost hands catch on nothing.
They can grasp neither the lapels of their enemies
nor the reason for this earthbound malingering.
The dead sleep fitfully on memorial benches,
in shop doorways and in libraries.
They gather around braziers in side streets.
The dead have heard the rumour
of a well of reviving waters –
an aqua vitae that conjures new bone,
new flesh, new nerves,
new tendons newly-stitched to new muscle.
Everywhere, they raise their translucent fists.

January 2017

Streets claggy with mud and wet leafmeal;
such steel grey skies, like we're living in a cloud,
and the news juggernaut keeps on rolling.
The people, we're told, have spoken,
though precisely what they've said's
for sale to the highest bidder.
Whatever it is sure is loud,
and History's awake with
one motherfucker of a headache,
looking for someone to kick.

My neighbour's children play in their garden,
learn the ebb and flow of 'I want,
but you seem to want more'.
Good kids. You guess they'll grow up right.
But will they have a chance? Like I did?
The first half of me's pre-web,
pre-international-public-shaming,
pre-GFC, monetised degrees,
house-price-hyper-inflation.

And one day, I guess, the servers will fail,
the online-avatar ghost-selves sink Lethe-wards
forever. We're still passing through is all,
and I recall staring wide-eyed
at the fiction shelves in the public library
I walked to weekly as a child,
thinking those books were
more permanent than me,
would see me out.
That was 1983.

Now I plant bulbs in January cold,
mud under my fingernails,
leafmeal in my boot-treads.
As it sinks in the west,
the winter sun throws a thin,
almost hopeful, splash of light
on the cankered rose by the wall.
But it's not even close.

First They Came . . .
after Martin Niemöller

First, the rains came hard as heart attacks:
tributaries, rivers swollen;
floodplains at sea for months.
And I did nothing because
I did not live on a floodplain.
But I saw the refugees on television,
cradling their confused dogs in dinghies,
paddling for higher ground,
their homes haunted by ghost flotillas
of tins and saucepans adrift on a brown tide
in their flooded kitchens.

Then, the hurricanes came so fast
they unspun meaning from their names,
and we had to coin new words
for storms that uprooted whole towns
from their east coast zip codes
like so many potato drills.
And I did nothing because
I did not live on America's eastern seaboard.
But I marvelled at YouTube videos
of houses imploding like punctured lungs.

When drought came to the Mediterranean
it came so often that farmers walked
away from their fields, were found
hanging from rafters
in barns even the rats had abandoned,
or were swept into shanties

like sirocco-blown dust
into the pith-craters of tangerines.
And I did nothing because
I did not live in southern Italy,
but I cursed the inflated price
of olives and chianti.

Rainforest became savannah;
I carved my imported rib-eye.
Reservoirs dried in southwestern Africa;
I hosed down my Range Rover.

And when the great ice-sheets calved,
and the seas rose like loaves –
those sundry states of emergency,
the peoples in diaspora,
the everyone-for-himself –
I did nothing because it was too late.

They are coming for me
in a frigate strewn with bones
heaving into view
from my penthouse balcony.
And there is no-one left to object.

Air Canada

Drinking the so-so
complimentary merlot
and reading
James Schuyler's *Last Poems*
in an aeroplane,
nearly 40,00 feet
above the Labrador Sea –
a bank of cloud like
Arctic tundra
stretching beneath us
as far as the crisp
cloud-horizon's
baby-blue.

How can something
this civilised
be so utterly
commonplace?
It should be a miracle
in anyone's book.
And not least because
it makes me think
why we haven't yet
managed to conquer
at least one or two
of our species' more
destructive limitations.

The Sign

For years I wore the sign above my head.
Shaped like a graphic novel's call-out,
and visible only to the town's eccentrics,
its long-term homeless, its trauma-tossed loons,
the sign often said something like:
This guy's worth stopping for a couple of quid.
Other times, I sensed it waxing more lyrically, viz:
This bloke has time for unsolicited conversation,
including rants against unknown nemeses.
If I was on a bus it might proclaim
to the bag-lady in the wheelchair nook:
This is the dude most likely to help you disembark
with those IKEA-blue sacks brimming with mildewed treasure.

The sign slowed me down in certain parts of town,
but I put up with its contingencies.
I worried it might be part of my soul,
that surgical removal of the sign –
even if such a thing were possible –
might diminish me irrevocably.
Secretly, I also feared it was preventing me
from fulfilling my potential.
It was hard to imagine the captains of industry
enduring such time-consuming nonsense.
Some sighed and told me their stories –
how they too had lived with inconvenient signs,
until they took back control.
The business card folded into my palm
with a reassuring stare
showed a man with a pair of oversized scissors

with which he has clearly just cut the umbilicus
joining a 'Mr Nice Guy' sign to his own head.
With his other hand he's waving a cheery farewell
as Monsieur N. G. floats off the edge of the card
like Gary Lockwood careening into space
in Kubrick's *2001*.

It took me a year to call the number.
The procedure's still misunderstood,
still somewhat niche.
I'd be happy to introduce you.
If it's something you'd like to pursue?

On Slow Time

Yes, it's all passing too quickly.
Middle age often says that,

pouring another thumb of bourbon.
And it's true that most everywhere

you'll find slowness fetishized, especially
in the always-sunlit purlieus of Adland –

the pyroclastic flow of gravy
over beef and potatoes,

a solitary 4×4 cruising a silver ribbon
of clear road through a National Park ...

It's this, more than the stuff itself,
we really want: time slowed.

To be here and absolutely nowhere else
so much it's like pulling the brakes

on Earth's back wheel. Or like
a Saturday morning forty Junes ago,

when you made the crest of the Heath,
stood astride your bicycle, and saw

the whole town frozen in the grip
of your, as yet, untested potential.

Interruption

I'd thrown a pan at our kitchen wall
and you were poised with the bread knife
when he first appeared in the hall
and we paused, briefly, to stare.
Loitering by the coat hooks,
a little Bertolt Brechtian man
with a teaspoon in his buttonhole
and a t-shirt that said INTERRUPTION.

Dust-motes hovered around him
like an aura in the slant of sunlight
beaming through our street door window nooks.

And in an earlier draft of this poem
I'd remind you of what happened next,
but now I'd prefer to consider
INTERRUPTION,
how he doesn't just punctuate
inevitable phases of inexorable narratives,
he diverts them, like culverts dug
by Napoleonic prisoners of war
re-routing a river from its course,
working their spades, watching
askance for the change of guard.

Faustian

In which you are a superannuated soldier
returning from war, your spoils (such as they are)
in threadbare pockets and canvas knapsack.

You're waymaking a desire line
between this crow-picked field
and a home that no longer exists.

Rest, now, on a milestone at the town's fringe –
filthy shirt cuffs, boot soles split, watch face cracked
like the hen's egg you'd kill for.

Call across memory for that blue-eyed,
ghost-haired boy who years ago whistled
from the high branches of edgeland trees.

Instead, the old man who's been watching,
side-saddle on the bough of a roadside elder,
jumps down, and approaches –

elbows a-jerk; knees like unbreeched rifles.
A hinged-paper silhouette by Jan Pieńkowski.
He uncurls one finger, pinning you to the landscape.

Question: what is it you most desire?
Proposal: and what will you give in return?
This, then, is your one chance: a moment

wherein the accumulated wisdom
of a turbulent life will be weighed
in the feather-light scales of your choice.

The town holds its breath.
A fox takes itself away into brown fields.
The blue-eyed boy is speaking with your mouth.

Magical Thinking

When you're eight it's not uncommon
to imagine your parents have died,
and to believe that's the reason
they haven't returned from work,
why there'll be a policeman at the door
any minute, with institutional eyes.

And if you find a perverse pleasure
in the imagined attention that follows,
in the Italian-restaurant-birthday-cake scale
of being all at once marked out by catastrophe;
and if your experience of this pleasure
coincides with the actual death of a parent,
well then, that there's a fuckup
of more than mere Larkinesque whimsy,
and a decent excuse for the wasted years.

I read somewhere that Coleridge
believed he'd killed his father
by means of magical thinking,
that the crack this opened in his psyche
only widened with time.
And you'd be surprised
how many of us wander the world,
Cain's mark on our foreheads –
bad-luck killers whose thought experiments
became coterminous
with actual mortal accident.
We shoulder that guilt.

We don't expect much.
We're so careful, even now,
what we wish for.

Response Time

He's halfway up the stairs, like a child
who's chosen an eccentric spot for a nap,
or a man camped at a hill station
the night before the final ascent.
Also clearly neither.
Clearly Jane's dad, Selwyn,
dead on the stairwell,
his little hand curled like a twig,
his face no longer his face.
Driving up, the house had seemed as always:
neatly-mown lawn, car on the drive,
curtains wide to the world.

I stoop to touch his shoulder. Sweet man.
'That's Jane, howling,' I think, as I turn
at the newel post to find her mum, Ellen,
skin wax-yellow, dead on the bedroom floor.
Was Selwyn responding to Ellen's cry,
hurrying up the stairs till his heart
burst like a wind-fallen plum?
Or did he walk unexpectedly
into eternity and she, perhaps,
waking from a nap,
looked down on his body,
knew the game was up,
retreated to her room to await the inevitable?

There's no point trying to resuscitate.
Death's been here,
lording it like some despot

who's been returned to power
in a farcical election.

We're standing in a moment
that's going to unfurl
in a great fathomless skein through our lives.
The phone's in my hand.
I do not know the name of the service I require.

Early Phases

Clearing his day room –
a bag of pills
in foil-wrapped packets.

～

Condolence cards.
An easterly wind
rattling the window frames.

～

Wind gusts on Small Water,
a skein of ashes,
mother and son turning home.

Infant Joy

His mother's blouse is the red of a desert sun
melting on the horizon, of a cigar-tip softly pulsing
in a Coen Brothers' extreme close-up.

Her perfume comes in waves not particles;
it's an Academy-Award-scale bouquet of gardenias;
it's sherbet in gold-rimmed glasses
on a terrace in Scheherazade's twilit garden.

Water's good too, of course. Water freshens every cell
like that long-imagined oasis the grounded pilot happens
     upon
while stumbling back across enemy lines
in an uncharted stretch of the Sahara.

And watch – he can move his hands, kick his feet.
Any kind of movement's Bastille Day.
Walking two steps then falling's a prison break
across two fields and a river on a June morning so clear
he can see his entire future.

Even closing his eyes against the sun
makes of his eyelids' interior cinema
a series of psychedelic pareidolia,

and the thoughts in his head, of course, are publishable.
Scratch that, they're an encyclopaedic history of
     consciousness
for Yale University Press
with a budget for full-colour illustrations.

Consciousness? It's amniotic.
A kind of bathtime for the soul, and

a teaspoon of mashed avocado's enough
to blow his tiny mind.

Five Daughters

When my life was placed between lawyers' lips,
to be blown in thin streams through caveats
and codicils, my eldest daughter furled in

like nightroses. And if she ditched my heart
among the serried aspens of a motorway embankment,
her twin drove B-roads all night, the radio

tuned to amnesia. Because he'd pickled my mind
in a jar, in his wunderkammer, my third girl
became a tour guide at the eccentric surgeon's

commemorative museum. But when I walked my soul
to the saltblown taffrail of a cross-Channel ferry,
to leave it there staring through night at the wake,

my penultimate child played slots till dawn
in the Deck 4 arcade. So, I know it's my youngest,
and most favoured, who'll startle that whicker

of memories I've become
from ancient woodland into a clearing
and the eager crosshairs of truth's opportune rifle.

Grandsongs

You came in a cold year.
Three of you.
The snows thick,
the woods loud
with opportunistic wolves.
And as mad-eyed liars
mounted podiums
in headline-sick towns
from Washington
to Westminster,
you tumbled
from your mothers
like fairytales.

16 JULY 2017

AMPUTEE SOLDIER PARACHUTES INTO RODEO
PACINO'S RESEMBLANCE TO DISGRACED FOOTBALL COACH
BIGGEST SNOWFALL IN DECADES BLANKETS CHILEAN CAPITAL

EVIL FELINE FINDS PERFECT MOMENT TO TRIP UP TODDLER
IS THERE SOMETHING FISHY ABOUT YOUR SUSHI?
COMATOSE FATHER PROVES HE'S NOT BRAIN-DEAD

HAIRDRESSING FIVE TIMES MORE DANGEROUS THAN CARPENTRY
HUMANS HARD-WIRED TO TILT HEADS WHEN KISSING
MINNEAPOLIS WOMAN SHOT DEAD IN HER PYJAMAS

I

The path's a path to somewhere known,
it cannot but be other –
desirelines scored by cautious feet
as brother follows brother.
But if you can hold terrain in mind
and trust to inwit's compass,
then leave the path, chart your course
out through the nodding crocus.

5 DECEMBER 2017

SUBURBAN NEW YORKERS FEAR COYOTE-WOLF HYBRID
HAWAIIAN WOMAN SEEKS RECORD FOR HUGE AVOCADO
WOMEN IN BURKAS GIVE 'NAZI MILO' THE FINGER

GOVERNOR TO DRUG-TEST FOOD-STAMP USERS
MIGRANT DINGHY REPLACES MANGER IN NATIVITY SCENE
FREEDOM CAUCUS BRUSH-BACK PITCH TO HOUSE LEADERS

[53]

'NIGELLA PINCHED RECIPE' SAYS EAGLE-EYED VIEWER
SENATORS WEIGH TRUMP'S USE OF POCAHONTAS
PENSION-VULTURES SWOOP ON OUR STEELWORKERS

II

A house in the forest is often a trap,
the witch's smile a lure;
town burghers watch each other's backs
so each can find his sinecure.
But if your will is firm and true
and you can read the weather,
there's almost nothing you can't do.
Be obstinate. Be clever.

14 DECEMBER 2017

DID SIR ISAAC NEWTON PREDICT NIBIRU?
ON THE OUTSIDE? BIG BEN. INSIDE? LEAKY LOOS
REJOICING REMOANERS GLOAT OVER BREXIT BETRAYAL

CHILD MIGRANTS TO BRITAIN ARE BALDING AND BEARDED
WOMEN UNHAPPIER THAN MEN TILL THEIR MID-80S
HOLLY AND HER JEDI BOOBS

FROM 'STRONG AND STABLE' TO THE MAYBOT
KILLING INTELLECTUALS IN THE SHADOW OF KISSINGER
THE SMELL OF DEATH STILL FILLS MOSUL

III

An exiled prince rides by and finds
a princess in a tower;
the misanthropic beast's redeemed
by girl exchanged for flower.
Love's not the object of a quest;
it has neither form nor weight.
You'll find it where you least expect,
by accident. Just wait.

Epilogue

And you, Forrest, eldest of four,
what shall I say to you?
Remember that the prophets
haven't stopped calling us back
from greed and stupidity,
from silken dalliance,
from tissued fripperies.
There's no last word,
no final statement –
the prophets keep on coming.
How else should we explain,
for example,
the late, great albums
of Leonard Cohen?
Revelation's emerging
always around us,

now – perhaps –
more than ever.
Put your ear up close
to the times.
Listen.

Nina

She wanted to be America's first
black classical pianist,
and America thought that
an adjective too far.
But she played on,
by any means necessary.

And listen to almost any recording,
but especially the version of 'Sinnerman'
on *Pastel Blues* from 1965,
and you'll hear it in every note,
right there in those last plaintive cries –
"Lord, Lord, hear me prayin'" –
in the furious, percussive piano:
the unbearable difference between
the sun on your face for a moment,
and one little tear in the Mississippi river
in a month of ceaseless rain.

According to Warren
her rider, latterly, was
sausages, Champagne, cocaine.

Lullaby

And when on the third night we woke again
to the irregular fricative refrain

of leathery wings careening into walls,
lampshades, bedheads, wardrobes –

the hapless determination of pipistrelles
circling inches above our pillowed heads
in the pitch black –

>black dreams
>who'd taken the form of bats,
>crawled from nests in our heads
>to unfurl their suggestions
>as they fledged into the room
>seeking the mosquito-thick
>skies of their night hunting –

we understood the cost of what eluded us.

Notes

VISION HELMET

was inspired by a sculpture called 'Helmet Mask', by David M. General. Permanent collection, Daphne Cockwell Gallery of Canada: First Peoples, Royal Ontario Museum, Toronto.

MYTHOLOGY

owes a clear and obvious debt to the short essay form pioneered by Roland Barthes in his famous book.

THE GAMES WE PLAY

was inspired by a short film by Francis Alÿs called *Reel-Unreel* (Afghan projects, 2010–2014), which I caught at AGO in Toronto.

TEACUPS

owes a debt to Henry Hobhouse's book *Seeds of Change: Six Plants that Transformed Mankind* (Papermac, 1995).

GRANDSONGS

makes use of a series of found headlines pertaining to the birth dates of three of my wife's four grandsons.

NINA

makes reference to a short fragment of dialogue between the versions of themselves played by Nick Cave and Warren Ellis in the film *20,000 Days on Earth* (directed by Forsyth and Pollard, 2014). For those with an interest in such things, the poem's early drafts were produced on my Silver-Reed SR 180 De Luxe typewriter, the same machine Cave uses in the film.

Acknowledgements

I am grateful to the editors of the following publications in which earlier versions of these poems first appeared: 'Other People', then known as 'Sauce for the Goose', in *Poetry London*. 'Five Daughters' in *Poetry Wales*. 'Newsworthy' and 'First They Came' in *International Times*. 'Vision Helmet' and 'In the Old Neighbourhood' in *Raceme*. 'Magical Thinking' in *The Moth*. 'Lullaby' in *Antiphon* (online). 'Late Electric Age' in *New Boots and Pantisocracies* (online). 'Early Phases' in *Blithe Spirit*. 'Five Lessons' in *Magma*. 'Quiddity', 'Haecceity', and 'Mythology' in *Hotel* (online).

'Five Lessons' also appears in *The Caught Habits of Language*, edited by Rachael Boast, Andy Ching and Nathan Hamilton (Donut Press, 2018). And a number of these poems also appear in a limited edition chapbook called *Vision Helmet* (Maquette Press, 2016), skilfully edited by Andy Brown.

'Newsworthy' was written as a commission piece for *The News Agents* on Resonance FM. 'First They Came' was written on commission for the Bristol Festival of Nature 2014.

I received excellent advice and incisive editorial comment from Rachael Boast, Jane Briggs, Andy Brown, Matthew Caley, Katy Evans-Bush and Andrew Jamison. I am grateful for a residency with Bristol University's Poetry Institute. Gratitude is also due to my employer, who gave me a sabbatical term in which I was able to bring the collection together.

NEW FICTION FROM SALT

NEW POETRY FROM SALT

KADDY BENYON
The Tidal Wife (978-1-78463-158-1)

AMIT CHAUDHURI
Sweet Shop (978-1-78463-182-6)

MATTHEW HAIGH
Death Magazine (978-1-78463-206-9)

ALLISON ADELLE HEDGE COKE (ED.)
Effigies III (978-1-78463-183-3)

KIRSTEN IRVING
Never Never Never Come Back (978-1-78463-156-7)

ANDREW MCDONNELL
The Somnambulist Cookbook (978-1-78463-199-4)

ELEANOR REES
The Well at Winter Solstice (978-1-78463-184-0)

JON STONE
School of Forgery (978-1-78463-087-4)

ANNA WOODFORD
Changing Room (978-1-78463-088-1)

This book has been typeset by
SALT PUBLISHING LIMITED
using Sabon, a font designed by Jan Tschichold
for the D. Stempel AG, Linotype and Monotype Foundries.
It is manufactured using Holmen Book Cream 70gsm,
a Forest Stewardship Council™ certified paper from the
Hallsta Paper Mill in Sweden. It was printed and bound
by Clays Limited in Bungay, Suffolk, Great Britain.

CROMER
GREAT BRITAIN
MMXIX